# Digging

A 40-Day Journey
Out of Who You Are

Devotional Book

By: Curtiss Cain

Copyright © 2020 by Curtiss Cain

All rights reserved.

No part of the author's contributions may be reproduced, transmitted or stored by any means; electronically, mechanically, photocopying, recording, scanning or otherwise without prior written consent from the author.

Where noted, copies of select pages may be made. Copies must be reproduced with no changes or alterations to words, page layout or artwork, except for meeting the requirement of all pages giving credit to the author.

Scripture quotations are taken from the Holy Bible, New Living Translation, copyright ©1996, 2004, 2007 by Tyndale House Foundation. Used by permission of Tyndale House Publishers, Inc., Carol Stream, Illinois 60188. All rights reserved.

# Contents

| | |
|---|---|
| Introduction | i |
| Week 1: Rediscovering Your True Identity | 1 |
| Week 2: Spiritual Preparation | 9 |
| Week 3: Discovering Your Gifts | 17 |
| Week 4: Unpacking Your Gifts | 25 |
| Week 5: Using Your Gifts in Daily Life | 33 |
| Week 6: Using Your Gifts as the Church | 41 |
| What's Next? | 47 |
| Spiritual Gifts Survey | 49 |
| Defining Your Spiritual Gifts | 53 |
| Answer Sheet | 58 |
| Acknowledgments | 61 |
| Bibliography | 62 |

# Introduction

"I've heard that God gives gifts to all believers, but I'm not sure what mine are, or to be honest, if I have any. If I do, I don't know how to find them and when I find them, what do I do with them?" Does any of this sound familiar to you? These are words I've heard so many times over the years. From teens who are excited to serve and new to faith, to beautiful 90+ year olds who have heard more sermons than I'll ever preach and can't remember not being in church. I have sat with a number of people, who in all vulnerability have shared feelings of wanting to be used by God but feel lost and unsure where to start. This all came to fullness when I was blessed to serve two churches, one after the other, where there was a genuine yearning to serve God more, a want to not just be administrative in how the church was run but to empower people within the church to do effective ministry. In short, they wanted to see God do wonderful things and they wanted to be a part of it. They wanted to be released into ministry, to find the kind of joy, empowerment and fulfillment they hear others talk about when it comes to living out of a confidence of knowing who God made them to be. They wanted serving to be more about *hope* (finding personal joy in building up the Kingdom of God) instead of *hand grenades* (someone, please dive on this administrative task to save the rest of us), but they weren't quite sure where to start.

Before moving on, we need to explore what spiritual gifts are not; they are not all the same. 1 Corinthians 12 talks about the fact that the human body is made of many parts; each part has its function. In the same way, for the body of Christ (the church) to fully function and do what it needs to, the diversity of each and every gift is needed and needs to come together. This helps us, because it sets us free from believing that to use our spiritual gifts means everyone must be comfortable talking to strangers about salvation or be inspired to stand in front of a large group and preach. No, God has given us all different gifts, designing us to find purpose in serving that fits our individual personalities best. As the one who designed you and knows you more than any other, God has hand chosen each and every one of your gifts to bring you great joy and fulfillment.

Now God will sometimes push us, he will nudge us to do something uncomfortable. The time you spend digging into your gifts over these next 40 days may make you uncomfortable at times as you wrestle with who God made you to be, but the only reason God pushes us to do more is because he believes in us. God sees potential in you to become even more than you already are, so there can be tension in exploring and even using your God-given gifts, good tension! Like guitar strings, if we allow God to tune each and every one of us individually, a beautiful song begins and if we allow the various instruments to work together, it becomes a sacred symphony the world wants to hear.

This is a 40-day study. The Bible teaches us there is a wholeness, a completion, even a refining to doing something 40 times. Christ was in the wilderness for 40 days, fasting and preparing for his public ministry (Matthew 4:1-11). God gave Nineveh 40 days to repent of their sins and they did (Jonah 3:1-5). On more than one occasion, Moses went up on a mountain and spent 40 days and 40 nights with God (Exodus 24:1-18, 24:1-35). The Israelites spent 40 years in the desert eating manna (bread from heaven), learning to trust in God again and follow his word (Exodus 16:33-35) and the list goes on.

As we begin, know this is not your typical devotional. Instead of a scripture, a short teaching and a question to ponder or scripted prayer, here you are given a scriptural theme for each day, several questions with room to write your answers and a closing prayer challenge. The reason is that this is a study of *self-exploration*, seeking to discover and understand what *you* think, how *you* feel and most of all, what gifts God has given *you*. In the same way, there are no "right" or "wrong" answers to these questions. Even if you've never picked up a Bible before, that's ok. The point is you already know you! You know how you think, what's important to you and what you are passionate about. You know what injustices weigh heavy on your heart and whom you feel compassion towards. Often our gifts, strengths and joys for serving are found through the things we already enjoy doing, dream about, or think about. Therefore, this devotional study will leave you a little extra space to dig deep within yourself, ask some fun and hard questions, and in doing so, hopefully challenge you to ask yourself what you find speaking into your own spiritual life. The hope is, instead of only focusing on giving you a teaching, you partner with the Holy Spirit and together, become your own teacher.

    As a final note, don't let the space provided for answers hinder you. Feel free to write as much or as little as you like. The only guideline is not to stop until you feel as if you have answered the question. Remember, this is your book, no one else's. Unless you let them, no one else will read this, so don't hold back! Feel free to be as blunt, honest, hopeful and genuine as possible.

# Week 1

## Rediscovering Your True Identity

With work, family, school, worries and bills we are often so overwhelmed with responsibilities and concerns that we have little, if any, time for ourselves. Add in social pressures to conform our personalities and we can end up spending so much time trying to become someone else, we can lose sight of who we are inside. Over this next week, you'll be invited to begin gently pulling back the layers you've built, rediscover what you like about yourself, perhaps remember some things that used to bring you joy and begin the process of falling in love with the person God made you to be.

**Day 1**

*¹ About that time the disciples came to Jesus and asked, "Who is greatest in the Kingdom of Heaven?"*
*² Jesus called a little child to him and put the child among them. ³ Then he said, "I tell you the truth, unless you turn from your sins and become like little children, you will never get into the Kingdom of Heaven. ⁴ So anyone who becomes as humble as this little child is the greatest in the Kingdom of Heaven.*
*⁵ "And anyone who welcomes a little child like this on my behalf is welcoming me.*
- *Matthew 18:1-5*

For many of us, there was a point in our lives when we felt the most like ourselves. For some this was before peer pressure, great responsibilities and busy lives. For others, it might be right now. When in your life did you feel you had the most permission to be yourself? What was it about that time that made you feel as if you could be yourself?

_____
_____

Describe that person. What was it you liked so much about yourself then? _____
_____

Write three traits about that person you would like to have back or hold on to for the rest of your life, (sense of humor, risk taker, brave...)?
   1. _____
   2. _____
   3. _____

**Closing Prayer:** Use your answers above to thank God for what you like about yourself.

## Day 2

*¹³ One day some parents brought their children to Jesus so he could lay his hands on them and pray for them. But the disciples scolded the parents for bothering him.*
*¹⁴ But Jesus said, "Let the children come to me. Don't stop them! For the Kingdom of Heaven belongs to those who are like these children." ¹⁵ And he placed his hands on their heads and blessed them before he left.*
- *Matthew 19:13-15*

There is a deep joy and authenticity in our blessings from God and sometimes those blessings are simply doing things that bring us happiness. When you felt most like yourself in life, what kinds of things did you like to do, (hobbies, activities...)?

_____

_____

Other times, those blessings come out of our spirit loving others in a way that is authentic to us. Even if it seems a little childish or silly now, during that time in your life, what did you enjoy doing for others (family, friends, neighbors, strangers...)? _____

_____

_____

How do you find joy in helping others today? This answer often begins to help us understand the gifts God has given to us.

_____

_____

**Closing Prayer:** Pray for three people you know who are in need, then ask God to use you to bless someone within the next 24 hours.

**Day 3**

¹³ *You made all the delicate, inner parts of my body
and knit me together in my mother's womb.*
¹⁴ *Thank you for making me so wonderfully complex!
Your workmanship is marvelous—how well I know it...*
¹⁷ *How precious are your thoughts about me, O God.
They cannot be numbered!*
¹⁸ *I can't even count them;
they outnumber the grains of sand!
And when I wake up,
you are still with me!*
- *Psalms 139:13, 14, 17 & 18*

Our gifts can often come out of how God designed us, so let's take a moment to explore who you are.

Using no more than five words, how would you describe yourself now? _____

Our identity should not come from what others think, but sometimes an outsider's perspective teaches us things about ourselves we might not have noticed. Using only five words, how do you think your friends would describe you?
_____
_____

Is the above answer different from how you see yourself?
_____

What are three of your strengths?
1. _____ 2. _____ 3. _____

What are three areas in which you need to grow?
1. _____ 2. _____ 3. _____

**Closing Prayer:** Thank God for your three strengths and ask for his help with your three growth areas.

## Day 4

*⁵ And you must love the Lord your God with all your heart, all your soul, and all your strength. ⁶ And you must commit yourselves wholeheartedly to these commands that I am giving you today. ⁷ Repeat them again and again to your children. Talk about them when you are at home and when you are on the road, when you are going to bed and when you are getting up.*

- *Deuteronomy 6:5-7*

There is a difference between trying to become something you're not and gleaning traits from others, melding them into your identity because it speaks to who you want to be. Who were some of the teachers, mentors and guides in your life you looked up to? What traits did they teach you through how they lived?

**Name**                          **Traits**

_____ : _____

_____

_____ : _____

_____

_____ : _____

_____

_____ : _____

_____

What kind of person do you want to be? _____

_____

_____

**Closing Prayer:** Thank God for the people you just wrote about and ask to be used by God to bless someone in the next 24 hours, so you may be that person for others.

# Day 5

*18 "So commit yourselves wholeheartedly to these words of mine. Tie them to your hands and wear them on your forehead as reminders. 19 Teach them to your children.*
- **Deuteronomy 11:18-19**

Often our experiences as a child shape our faith journey and views of God, both good and bad, whether we grew up going to church or not. As a child, what was your impression of church?

_____
_____
_____
_____
_____

As a child, what was your impression of God? _____

_____
_____
_____
_____

Has your view of church and God changed? If so, how?

_____
_____
_____
_____

**Closing Prayer:** Think about Jesus' personality, the things he did, how he acted, the people he spent time with, what he taught, the ways he helped. What is it about the example Jesus lived that connects with your heart? Thank him for it.

## Day 6

*¹¹ "For I know the plans I have for you," says the Lord. "They are plans for good and not for disaster, to give you a future and a hope.*
- *Jeremiah 29:11*

God gives spiritual gifts to all believers for the building up of his church and for the healing of a broken world. In addition, out of love God also gives all people what is sometimes referred to as 'birthrights' or 'talents.' No matter how small you think they are, or how good or bad you may believe you are at it, what are some of the things that have always come easier to you than others (music, art, leading, serving, listening, sports, hobbies, working with your hands…)? In other words, what are your talents? Don't write 'none.' These can sometimes be indicators of your spiritual gifts.

_____
_____

One of the things that tries to rob us of our true identity is the expectations others put on us and the self-inflicted expectations we feel we must live up to. What, if any are some of the expectations in your life right now that don't allow you to live into your true identity? _____
_____

What would need to happen for you to start living into your true identity more? What would you need to let go of, stop doing or even start doing? Is there someone or a group of people whose opinions you need to value less?

_____
_____

**Closing Prayer:** Tell God what kind of person you want to be.

**Day 7**

*1 There was a man named Nicodemus, a Jewish religious leader who was a Pharisee. 2 After dark one evening, he came to speak with Jesus. "Rabbi," he said, "we all know that God has sent you to teach us. Your miraculous signs are evidence that God is with you."*
*3 Jesus replied, "I tell you the truth, unless you are born again, you cannot see the Kingdom of God."*
*4 "What do you mean?" exclaimed Nicodemus. "How can an old man go back into his mother's womb and be born again?"*
*5 Jesus replied, "I assure you, no one can enter the Kingdom of God without being born of water and the Spirit.*
- *John 3:1-5*

In our true identity, God gifts us with traits and talents that help not only form who we are but help us find joy and fulfillment. Spiritual gifts are those gifts we receive upon accepting Christ in our hearts, being born again of the Spirit, if you will. These gifts allow us to find a deeper sense of who we are and fulfillment in serving God through his church. In a few words, write your understanding of these spiritual gifts.

Teaching: _____

Encouragement: _____

Generosity: _____

Leadership: _____

**Closing Prayer:** Think of one person who did something kind for you recently. Thank God for them and their act of kindness.

# Week 2

## Spiritual Preparation

The best way to get stronger is to pick up something heavy over and over again. More so, the most effective way to get stronger, is to pick up something heavy enough that we may get a bit uncomfortable, even a bit sore. Before we can bless others and use our gifts, we need to prepare our hearts and souls for the task ahead. Like cultivating soil, gently and lovingly turning it up, adding nutrients, water and preparing it for the seed, this yields a fuller harvest than just putting the seed in any old dirt. This week is about spiritual formation, your personal relationship with God. Go into this with an open heart and mind towards what God would have you explore, know and experience..

# Day 8

*¹⁶ So I say, let the Holy Spirit guide your lives. Then you won't be doing what your sinful nature craves. ¹⁷ The sinful nature wants to do evil, which is just the opposite of what the Spirit wants. And the Spirit gives us desires that are the opposite of what the sinful nature desires. These two forces are constantly fighting each other, so you are not free to carry out your good intentions.*
- *Galatians 5:16-17*

There are several things that can hinder us from living in or even using our spiritual gifts. One of those is the battle we all face between what our *sinful nature craves* and what our *spirit wants*. Often the first step is recognizing those things we need to begin moving away from. What are some of the things your sinful nature craves that you need to begin getting away from? In other words, what wrong actions, thoughts or attitudes do you struggle with most often?

_____

_____

These wrong actions, thoughts and attitudes are what we call sin, but besides sin there are other things that can hinder us from being the kind of person our spirit wants to be. If we're not careful, worries, conflicts, stress or depression can dominate our thoughts, attitudes and actions. Is there anything else happening in your life right now that's driving a wedge between you and God? _____

_____

Looking at the two questions above, what first steps do you need to take to start moving away from these things?

_____

_____

**Closing Prayer:** Looking at all you've written today, ask God for strength where you need it and forgiveness for wrongs you've done.

## Day 9

[19] *When you follow the desires of your sinful nature, the results are very clear: sexual immorality, impurity, lustful pleasures,* [20] *idolatry, sorcery, hostility, quarreling, jealousy, outbursts of anger, selfish ambition, dissension, division,* [21] *envy, drunkenness, wild parties, and other sins like these. Let me tell you again, as I have before, that anyone living that sort of life will not inherit the Kingdom of God.*
[22] *But the Holy Spirit produces this kind of fruit in our lives: love, joy, peace, patience, kindness, goodness, faithfulness,* [23] *gentleness, and self-control. There is no law against these things!*

- *Galatians 5:19-23*

In continuing to explore this battle between our sinful nature and spiritual wants, what we need to remember is, when we take one thing out of our lives it leaves a gap, whether that is a gap in how our time is spent or in our emotional fulfillment. If we don't purposefully fill that gap, Satan will fill it for us when we don't notice and with something we definitely don't want. For your spiritual growth, in serving others or simple self-improvement, what are three areas you want to grow in?

1. _____
2. _____
3. _____

**Closing Prayer:** For the rest of your devotional time today take a few minutes to talk to God about these things. Try to answer each of the following questions. Why do you want these things in your life? Why are they important to you? What do you think would be hard about living into them? What good could come out of these?

## Day 10

*¹ "I am the true grapevine, and my Father is the gardener. ² He cuts off every branch of mine that doesn't produce fruit, and he prunes the branches that do bear fruit so they will produce even more. ³ You have already been pruned and purified by the message I have given you. ⁴ Remain in me, and I will remain in you. For a branch cannot produce fruit if it is severed from the vine, and you cannot be fruitful unless you remain in me.*

- *John 15:1-4*

Being pruned by God can seem scary and even painful. It's the unknown of what he will do or because we know exactly what he will prune away if we let him. Do you have any fears of what God might do in your pruning process? What might he prune away if you let him? _____
_____
_____

Sometimes pruning isn't as much about a noticeable sin as it can be a way we portray ourselves to others that isn't true to who we really are, that is, our true identity. Is there anywhere in your life you portray yourself to be someone you're not?
_____
_____

Answering in vulnerability, what are you afraid would happen if you give these up? Would you fear people would think about you differently? What pressure do you feel to hold on to these things (from others or yourself)? _____
_____
_____

**Closing Prayer:** Believing the person God made you to be will bring you more joy and fulfillment than trying to live up to others' expectations. Take a moment to thank God for the things you like about yourself.

## Day 11

*⁵ "Yes, I am the vine; you are the branches. Those who remain in me, and I in them, will produce much fruit. For apart from me you can do nothing. ⁶ Anyone who does not remain in me is thrown away like a useless branch and withers. Such branches are gathered into a pile to be burned. ⁷ But if you remain in me and my words remain in you, you may ask for anything you want, and it will be granted! ⁸ When you produce much fruit, you are my true disciples. This brings great glory to my Father.*

- *John 15:5-8*

Often when pruning happens, it redirects nourishment to the fruit and allows the roots to grow deeper. Can you think of a time in your life God pruned something away from you and it made you stronger? What happened? _____

_____

Sometimes we can fear what it would look like to *produce much fruit* because we don't know what God might call us to do or how far he might call us outside of our comfort zone. Yet often those moments can produce the sweetest spiritual fruit in our lives. Can you think of a time God called you out of your comfort zone? What happened? _____

_____

_____

Do you have any fears in discovering your spiritual gifts or in what God might call you to do? If so, it's ok to name those! What do you fear God might call you to do? _____

_____

_____

**Closing Prayer:** Knowing that God only gives us challenges to make us better, think of a moment where God purified you. Tell him how you've been changed by that and thank him for it.

**Day 12**

⁴ *Love is patient and kind. Love is not jealous or boastful or proud* ⁵ *or rude. It does not demand its own way. It is not irritable, and it keeps no record of being wronged.* ⁶ *It does not rejoice about injustice but rejoices whenever the truth wins out.* ⁷ *Love never gives up, never loses faith, is always hopeful, and endures through every circumstance.*
- **1 Corinthians 13:4-7**

Verbs are action words, something you can do, and this scripture is packed with them (patient, kind, jealous, boastful, proud, love…). Read the scripture again. Are there any you struggle with doing?

_____ , _____ , _____

Sometimes we focus so much on our areas of growth we almost fear talking about our strengths because we don't want to seem boastful, but it can be just as important! If we don't own them, we miss out on some of the key attributes that make us who we are. Read the scripture again. What areas do you shine in?

_____ , _____ , _____

Read the scripture one more time, look for several traits in the list you would like to model your life after (don't just say "all of them," but are there any you would like to stand out above the rest throughout your life).

_____ , _____ , _____

**Closing Prayer:** Ask for God's help modeling the traits you just listed, be specific about how you would like these to be a part of your life. What would you like to do with them? Whom in your life would you want to treat differently?

## Day 13

*⁴ He [Christ] did this so that the just requirement of the law would be fully satisfied for us, who no longer follow our sinful nature but instead follow the Spirit.*

- *Romans 8:4*

Christ has paid our debt and set us free from the control of sin, but we are still imperfect beings, with a sinful past, living in a sinful world and those chains don't like to let go! While we cannot be controlled by sin, we can still be influenced by it. With what temptations do you struggle with? _____

_____

Our relationship with God is a two-way street. While Christ paid for our sins, we still need to own them and seek his forgiveness. Is there anything you need to confess before God and repent of? _____

_____

At times, it can be easier to offer forgiveness to others than it is to forgive ourselves. If we earnestly repent of our sins, Christ *will* forgive us, but we can often struggle with fully accepting it. Whether it's something that happened years ago or recently, is there anything you have repented of but haven't forgiven yourself of? _____

_____

**Closing Prayer:** Sometimes letting go of something isn't as easy as just saying "I will." A great first step is claiming the fact that through Christ, we *are* forgiven! Look over your answers above. Read the scripture again. Pray specifically over those things and ask his forgiveness. When you're finished, claim your freedom and write below "*in the name of Jesus Christ, I am forgiven!*"

_____

# Day 14

²² *You were cleansed from your sins when you obeyed the truth, so now you must show sincere love to each other as brothers and sisters. Love each other deeply with all your heart.*
- 1 Peter 1:22

Many things pull us back from being close to God and in so doing, prevent us from becoming the person he made us to be. Is there anyone you harbor anger towards or resentment? Why, what happed? _____
_____
_____

Is there anyone you need to forgive? _____
_____
_____

Is there anyone you need to ask forgiveness of or reconcile a relationship with? What do you need to do? _____
_____
_____
_____

**Closing Prayer:** Forgive and forget is not only unbiblical but encourages us to ignore the fact that some people are poisonous and will continue to be poisonous in our lives. To truly forgive someone is to want the best for them. The key is the intention of your heart. In your prayer, take a moment to offer others forgiveness if you need to and seek God's guidance for reconciliation if you need the forgiveness of someone else.

# Week 3

## Discovering Your Gifts

This is the moment you've been waiting for! or is it? As you reflect on all you've written about yourself, your true identity, what we called your birthrights (the talents God gave you) and the ways you already find joy in serving, you may already have an idea of what your gifts may be. In this chapter, on day 16, you'll have the opportunity to take a spiritual gifts survey, which may either confirm your suspicions or challenge you to consider a new gift that may be within you. Remember though, the most accurate spiritual gifts survey is your own thoughts, passions, concerns of injustice and experience finding fulfillment in servanthood.

## Day 15

Spiritual gifts are God's gift to all believers for the building up and care of the church, for bringing healing to a broken world and helping each person find where they may be called to serve in the community of believers. One tool for discovering our gifts is reading them in scripture and asking ourselves which one(s) we feel best describes us.

Below are three places the Bible specifically lists spiritual gifts. Be aware that your translation may use slightly different words to describe each gift. Read the scriptures below and, as you do, consider the first two questions.

*Romans 12:6-8, 1 Corinthians 12:7-31 & Ephesians 4:11-13*

What three spiritual gifts do you feel describe you best?

_____ , _____ , _____

What three spiritual gifts do you feel are not you?

_____ , _____ , _____

Can you see any of these gifts in other believers you know? Who and which ones? _____

_____

**Closing Prayer:** Over this next week, just talk to God about the things on your heart. Thank God for something. Ask for guidance, strength, clarity, whatever you need.

## Day 16

[3] Because of the privilege and authority God has given me, I give each of you this warning: Don't think you are better than you really are. Be honest in your evaluation of yourselves, measuring yourselves by the faith God has given us. [4] Just as our bodies have many parts and each part has a special function, [5] so it is with Christ's body. We are many parts of one body, and we all belong to each other.

[6] In his grace, God has given us different gifts for doing certain things well. So if God has given you the ability to prophesy, speak out with as much faith as God has given you. [7] If your gift is serving others, serve them well. If you are a teacher, teach well. [8] If your gift is to encourage others, be encouraging. If it is giving, give generously. If God has given you leadership ability, take the responsibility seriously. And if you have a gift for showing kindness to others, do it gladly.

- *Romans 12:3-8*

**Turn to page 49 and complete the Spiritual Gifts Survey.**

When taking a spiritual gifts survey, it is not uncommon to have a group of about 1-3 gifts that stand out above the rest. These are not concrete, but *indicators* of where God might be calling you to serve in the church. List those gifts below.

_____   _____   _____

Are you surprised at any of them? Do you feel they accurately describe you? _____

_____

Can you see anywhere in your life where you've used these gifts formally or informally in serving others? If so, how? ___

_____

**Closing Prayer:** Over this week, just talk to God about the things on your heart. Thank God for something. Ask for guidance, strength, clarity, whatever you need.

## Day 17

*¹⁶ So don't be misled, my dear brothers and sisters. ¹⁷ Whatever is good and perfect is a gift coming down to us from God our Father, who created all the lights in the heavens. He never changes or casts a shifting shadow. ¹⁸ He chose to give birth to us by giving us his true word. And we, out of all creation, became his prized possession.*

- ***James 1:16-18***

In addition to the primary gifts God gives us for serving him through the church, he can also give us gifts that change depending on the needs and seasons of our lives. In your spiritual gifts survey, you may notice a second grouping of about 1-3 gifts that closely follow the first. Again, these are not concrete, but *indicators* of seasonal gifts in your life. List those gifts below.

_____  _____  _____

Are you surprised at any of these gifts? Do you feel they describe you, your life, or the needs of others around you right now? _____
_____
_____
_____

Even in a small way, can you think of any way you are using these gifts in your life? If so, how? _____
_____
_____
_____

**Closing Prayer:** Over this week, just talk to God about the things on your heart. Thank God for something. Ask for guidance, strength, clarity, whatever you need.

## Day 18

⁹ *But you are not like that, for you are a chosen people. You are royal priests, a holy nation, God's very own possession. As a result, you can show others the goodness of God, for he called you out of the darkness into his wonderful light.*
¹⁰ *"Once you had no identity as a people;*
*now you are God's people.*
*Once you received no mercy;*
*now you have received God's mercy."*
- *1 Peter 2:9,10*

As followers of Christ, scripture tells us we are all called to the royal priesthood, through servant ministry. This does not mean we are all called to be pastors, but to use the unique gifts God has given each of us in caring for other believers and ministering to a hurting, broken and lost world on Christ's behalf. How do you feel about being called to ministry?

_____
_____
_____
_____

If you had an unlimited amount of time, money and resources at your disposal, what would you love to do that would make a positive difference in the world? _____

_____
_____
_____
_____

**Closing Prayer:** Over this week, just talk to God about the things on your heart. Thank God for something. Ask for guidance, strength, clarity, whatever you need.

**Day 19**

*[10] God has given each of you a gift from his great variety of spiritual gifts. Use them well to serve one another.*
- **1 Peter 4:10**

Though we are not all meant to have the same spiritual gifts, sometimes Christians can feel as if all devout believers "should" have one or more of the same gifts. Looking over your spiritual gifts survey answer sheet, list the gifts you might feel bad about not having, or wish you had?

_____
_____

As important as it is to discover your gifts, it can also be freeing to know which gifts God has *not* given you. Be aware, there is a difference between growth areas and areas we simply do not feel called to. Look over the spiritual gifts answer sheet again. Are there any gifts God might not want you to have right now? What are they?

_____
_____

In remembering who you are and who you want to be, go back to Day 1. Write the three personality traits from your true identity that you wanted to keep your whole life. How do you still use these traits today?

1. _____ : _____
_____

2. _____ : _____
_____

3. _____ : _____
_____

**Closing Prayer:** Over this week, just talk to God about the things on your heart. Thank God for something. Ask for guidance, strength, clarity, whatever you need.

## Day 20

*⁷ "Keep on asking, and you will receive what you ask for. Keep on seeking, and you will find. Keep on knocking, and the door will be opened to you. ⁸ For everyone who asks, receives. Everyone who seeks, finds. And to everyone who knocks, the door will be opened.*
- *Matthew 7:7,8*

All spiritual gifts surveys are only an indicator of your gifts. Look over your gifts from Day 16 again. If you did not score high in a gift, that doesn't mean you won't or can't have it. Are there any gifts you did not score high in that you would like to explore or develop? _____
_____
_____

Though we often have several gifts God gives us for most of our lives, spiritual gifts can change over time. If you have taken a spiritual gifts survey in the past, how do the results of this one compare? If not, skip this question. _____
_____
_____

Is there anything about the gifts you scored high in that make you feel uncomfortable? If so, what makes you uncomfortable about it? _____
_____
_____

**Closing Prayer:** Over this week, just talk to God about the things on your heart. Thank God for something. Ask for guidance, strength, clarity, whatever you need.

# Day 21

*⁵ If you need wisdom, ask our generous God, and he will give it to you. He will not rebuke you for asking. ⁶ But when you ask him, be sure that your faith is in God alone. Do not waver, for a person with divided loyalty is as unsettled as a wave of the sea that is blown and tossed by the wind.*
- ***James 1:5,6***

We tend to understand things better when we explain them ourselves. Below list your 1-3 primary gifts, use the "Defining Your Spiritual Gifts" section on page 53, and in your own words explain what each one means.

_____: _____

_____: _____

_____: _____

Below list your 1-3 secondary gifts, use the "Defining Your Spiritual Gifts" section on page 53 and, in your own words explain what each one means.

_____: _____

_____: _____

_____: _____

**Closing Prayer:** Over this week, just talk to God about the things on your heart. Thank God for something. Ask for guidance, strength, clarity, whatever you need.

# Week 4

## Unpacking Your Gifts

Now that you've identified and begun to define your spiritual gifts, let's go one step further. Throughout this chapter you'll be encouraged to explore your gifts through scripture, spiritual discipline and practical understanding. You're going to give yourself good advice about each of your gifts. As you begin this week, you're going to be challenged to write your answers, not from the perspective of talking to yourself, but as if you're writing to a friend who has these gifts. *What advice, cautions, affirmations and encouragement would you give them?* Sometimes, the best advice for us to receive, is the kind of advice we would give someone we care about.

Our greatest source of information and direction from God comes from his Holy Word, the Bible. Over the next three days I invite you to choose three spiritual gifts that represent you most (they can be from your list of primary gifts, or not). In the back of many Bibles there is a "Concordance" or "Bible Dictionary." This is a scripture-based word search, helping you find where scripture talks about these words. Search your spiritual gift and words related to it (e.g. serving/helps: servant, servanthood, helper, helping). You can also do an internet search, www.openbible.info/topics and www.biblegateway.com are good resources. Just type the word in the search bar at the top of the website. Each day find three scriptures that explain, teach or give examples of your spiritual gift. Find scriptures you would share with a friend if they wanted to know more about that gift, then write out that scripture in your own words.

# Day 22

*¹ Now, dear brothers and sisters, regarding your question about the special abilities the Spirit gives us. I don't want you to misunderstand this. ² You know that when you were still pagans, you were led astray and swept along in worshiping speechless idols. ³ So I want you to know that no one speaking by the Spirit of God will curse Jesus, and no one can say Jesus is Lord, except by the Holy Spirit.*
- *1 Corinthians 12:1-3*

See page 25 for instructions.

First Gift: _____

| Scripture | What did you find? |
|---|---|
| _____: | _____ |
| _____: | _____ |
| _____: | _____ |

**Closing Prayer:** Thank God for this spiritual gift in your life, then based on the scriptures you just found and what you just learned, ask for guidance to live into this gift more.

## Day 23

*⁴ There are different kinds of spiritual gifts, but the same Spirit is the source of them all. ⁵ There are different kinds of service, but we serve the same Lord. ⁶ God works in different ways, but it is the same God who does the work in all of us.*
- ***1 Corinthians 12:4-6***

See page 25 for instructions.

Second Gift: _____

    Scripture               What did you find?

_____: _____
_____
_____: _____
_____
_____: _____
_____

**Closing Prayer:** Thank God for this spiritual gift in your life, then based on the scriptures you just found and what you just learned, ask for guidance to live into this gift more.

**Day 24**

⁷ *A spiritual gift is given to each of us so we can help each other.* ⁸ *To one person the Spirit gives the ability to give wise advice; to another the same Spirit gives a message of special knowledge.* ⁹ *The same Spirit gives great faith to another, and to someone else the one Spirit gives the gift of healing.* ¹⁰ *He gives one person the power to perform miracles, and another the ability to prophesy. He gives someone else the ability to discern whether a message is from the Spirit of God or from another spirit. Still another person is given the ability to speak in unknown languages, while another is given the ability to interpret what is being said.* ¹¹ *It is the one and only Spirit who distributes all these gifts. He alone decides which gift each person should have.*
- **1 Corinthians 12:7-11**

See page 25 for instructions.

Third Gift: _____

| Scripture | What did you find? |
|---|---|
| _____ : | _____ |
| _____ : | _____ |
| _____ : | _____ |

**Closing Prayer:** Thank God for this spiritual gift in your life, then based on the scriptures you just found and what you just learned, ask for guidance to live into this gift more.

## Day 25

*¹ So we must listen very carefully to the truth we have heard, or we may drift away from it. ² For the message God delivered through angels has always stood firm, and every violation of the law and every act of disobedience was punished. ³ So what makes us think we can escape if we ignore this great salvation that was first announced by the Lord Jesus himself and then delivered to us by those who heard him speak? ⁴ And God confirmed the message by giving signs and wonders and various miracles and gifts of the Holy Spirit whenever he chose.*
   -   ***Hebrews 2:1-4***

Using those same three spiritual gifts, answer each question as if you were talking to a friend who came to you for advice.

First Gift: _____

How would you explain this gift to a friend? _____
_____

How could someone use this gift to serve others? _____
_____

What should someone with this gift be cautious of? Could this create space for ego, or to be taken advantage of?
_____
_____

If your friend asked what *you* would most like to do to serve God and others with this gift, what would you tell them?
_____
_____


**Closing Prayer:** Pray over the needs and concerns of those in the world whom you mentioned in the last question.

**Day 26**

¹⁵ *Well then, since God's grace has set us free from the law, does that mean we can go on sinning? Of course not!* ¹⁶ *Don't you realize that you become the slave of whatever you choose to obey? You can be a slave to sin, which leads to death, or you can choose to obey God, which leads to righteous living.*
- *Romans 6:15-16*

Using those same three spiritual gifts, answer each question as if you were talking to a friend who came to you for advice.

Second Gift: _____

How would you explain this gift to a friend? _____
_____

How could someone use this gift to serve others? _____
_____

What should someone with this gift be cautious of? Could this create space for ego, or to be taken advantage of?
_____
_____

If your friend asked what *you* would most like to do to serve God and others with this gift, what would you tell them?
_____
_____

**Closing Prayer:** Pray over the needs and concerns of those in the world whom you mentioned in the last question.

## Day 27

*⁵ I remember your genuine faith, for you share the faith that first filled your grandmother Lois and your mother, Eunice. And I know that same faith continues strong in you. ⁶ This is why I remind you to fan into flames the spiritual gift God gave you when I laid my hands on you. ⁷ For God has not given us a spirit of fear and timidity, but of power, love, and self-discipline.*
- *2 Timothy 1:5-7*

Using those same three spiritual gifts, answer each question as if you were talking to a friend who came to you for advice.

Third Gift: _____

How would you explain this gift to a friend? _____
_____

How could someone use this gift to serve others? _____
_____

What should someone with this gift be cautious of? Could this create space for ego, or to be taken advantage of?
_____
_____

If your friend asked what *you* would most like to do to serve God and others with this gift, what would you tell them?
_____
_____

**Closing Prayer:** Pray over the needs and concerns of those in the world whom you mentioned in the last question.

**Day 28**

$^{28}$ And we know that God causes everything to work together for the good of those who love God and are called according to his purpose for them. $^{29}$ For God knew his people in advance, and he chose them to become like his Son, so that his Son would be the firstborn among many brothers and sisters.
- Romans 8:28, 29

Back on Day 7 you wrote about your understanding of the gifts below. Go back and read your definitions. Have they changed? Write your definition of each gift below. If you have one or more of the spiritual gifts mentioned here, feel free to substitute it with another gift you haven't been exploring this last week (see page 53).

Teaching: _____
_____

Encouragement: _____
_____

Generosity: _____
_____

Leadership: _____
_____

**Closing Prayer:** Think of one person who did something kind for you recently. Thank God for them and their act of kindness.

# Week 5

## Using Your Gifts in Daily Life

Taking care of ourselves is very important, but in order to fully live into our spiritual gifts our attitude, thoughts and actions should be focused on the needs of others. When we feel overwhelmed, stressed or distant from God, one of the most powerful steps we can take is simply finding just one person to serve. This not only challenges us to stop solely focusing on ourselves, but in serving we find a deepened and sacred sense of closeness with God, closeness with others and fulfillment as we care for others on behalf of our God.

**Day 29**

*⁹ Don't just pretend to love others. Really love them. Hate what is wrong. Hold tightly to what is good. ¹⁰ Love each other with genuine affection, and take delight in honoring each other.*
- *Romans 12:9,10*

Using the spiritual gifts God has given you in everyday life is central to finding joy and fulfillment, because it is centered on relationship; relationship with each other and with our creator. The foundation of positive relationships is making the conscious choice to focus on the good and potential in others. The problem is, whether it's our spouse, kids, friends, classmates or co-workers, we don't always focus on the good. As a result, our relationships with those we should serve most suffers. List three people you're glad are in your life. What positive attributes make them special to you?

_____ : _____

_____ : _____

_____ : _____

Often, the first step in building positive relationships with someone we don't particularly like is shifting our mindset about them. List three people you don't get along with well. What positive attributes do you see in them?

_____ : _____

_____ : _____

_____ : _____

**Closing Prayer:** Thank God for all six people by name. Pray God's goodness for their lives.

## Day 30

*[11]* *Never be lazy, but work hard and serve the Lord enthusiastically. [12] Rejoice in our confident hope. Be patient in trouble, and keep on praying. [13] When God's people are in need, be ready to help them. Always be eager to practice hospitality.*
- *Romans 12:11-13*

Living out our primary gifts is a wonderful way to serve our God and others, but it is not the only way. Though we may have some gifts we're better at than others, we are all called to serve in whatever way or place the Lord calls us. This is what it means to be obedient to God through servanthood.

*Evangelism* and *Teaching* can at times simply be sharing with others what God has done for you. What is it about knowing Christ that gives you confidence and hope?

_____
_____

*Encouragement* and *Faith* can be sharing the good God is doing in us and around us, the reasons we have for enthusiastically serving our Lord. What can you thank God for today? _____
_____

*Helps* and *Mercy* can be spread when we notice the needs of others and do something about it. Big or small, what is one need in someone's life you can meet within the next 24 hours? _____
_____

Within the next 24 hours, work to meet that need.


**Closing Prayer:** Some spiritual gifts may come easy to us, others we may be uncomfortable try. Ask God for help with at least one spiritual gift you're uncomfortable with and tell him what makes you uncomfortable about it.

# Day 31

*15 Be happy with those who are happy, and weep with those who weep. 16 Live in harmony with each other. Don't be too proud to enjoy the company of ordinary people. And don't think you know it all!*
- *Romans 12:15-16*

Whether it's how we were taught as children or preconceived notions, if we are not careful, we can lack respect for others by lumping whole groups of people together. Perhaps it's those of other cultures, languages, age groups, economic status, skin color - the list goes on. Are there any groups, even in small ways, for whom you lack respect? If so, who are they? _____

What is it about your understanding, experience or upbringing that lead you to feel this way? _____

Fear and discomfort are two of the greatest enemies of serving others, but compassion and love are two of the greatest enemies of fear. Further, trying to understand someone is the first step in moving toward love and compassion. What struggles do you think the people you just listed regularly face (emotional, economic, social, etc.)? _____

What positive attributes do you see in these people, or what hopes do you think they hold? _____

**Closing Prayer:** Regardless of life choices, take a moment to thank God for these people, as being beautifully and wonderfully made in the image of God.

## Day 32

*17 Never pay back evil with more evil. Do things in such a way that everyone can see you are honorable. 18 Do all that you can to live in peace with everyone.*
- **Romans 12:17,18**

What does it mean to you to live an honorable life in the eyes of God? _____
_____

What does it mean to you to honor your family? _____
_____
_____

What does it mean to you to honor a friendship? _____
_____
_____

What's one place in your life you need to strength to live a more honorable life in the eyes of God? _____
_____

**Closing Prayer:** Tell God what kind of man or woman of faith you would like to be and ask him for the strength to live into it.

# Day 33

*19 Dear friends, never take revenge. Leave that to the righteous anger of God. For the Scriptures say,*
*"I will take revenge; I will pay them back," says the Lord.*
*20 Instead, "If your enemies are hungry, feed them. If they are thirsty, give them something to drink. In doing this, you will heap burning coals of shame on their heads."*
*21 Don't let evil conquer you, but conquer evil by doing good.*
- *Romans 12:19-21*

Is there any one person or persons in your life who might fall under the category of "enemy," even in a small way?

_____

_____

Nowhere in scripture are we told to forgive and forget, but to truly forgive someone we need to hope God's goodness into their lives. If they've hurt you, have you forgiven them? Are you able to ask for God's goodness in their lives? If not, what would need to happen for you to be able to?

_____

_____

Whether it's praying God's goodness into their lives, a conversation (if it's appropriate), offering a simple smile or a kind word, how might God be calling you to make peace?

_____

_____

_____

**Closing Prayer:** God softens us and begins to set us free when we pray over our enemies. Ask God to bless the person or persons you just wrote about.

## Day 34

*$^{16}$ For you are free, yet you are God's slaves, so don't use your freedom as an excuse to do evil. $^{17}$ Respect everyone, and love the family of believers.*

- *1 Peter 2:16-17a*

Once we are free from fear and being consumed by what others think of us, our gifts often shine brightest when they are partnered with our passions. Below are some questions that may help you begin identifying your passions.

If you had $1 million and had to use it to help others, what would you spend it on? _____
_____

Where do you see potential for growth, healing, or joy in your community? _____
_____

If you could start a new ministry at your church and had an endless supply of volunteers, time and resources, what would you do? _____
_____

Where do you see brokenness in our nation that needs Christ's healing? _____
_____

**Closing Prayer:** Choose one of your answers and take a little time to pray over the people currently being affected by the problems you want to help resolve. Then, ask God to show you how you can be a part of that healing, even if it is in a small way.

**Day 35**

*⁸ Most important of all, continue to show deep love for each other, for love covers a multitude of sins. ⁹ Cheerfully share your home with those who need a meal or a place to stay. ¹⁰ God has given each of you a gift from his great variety of spiritual gifts. Use them well to serve one another.*
- *1 Peter 4:8-10*

Exploring our gifts to the best of our ability is good and helpful. It challenges us to think of serving in ways we may not have, or to ask some good questions that make us think, but we must also remember not to make it more complicated than it needs to be. Christ's message was simple. Follow him, love God, love others and let them love you back. Most people who find joy and fulfillment in serving others through their gifts, do so simply by being neighborly, loving on their kids or just trying to be a nice person. Today we're going to try and keep things simple as well.

Name two people you know who could use some kindness in their life? _____
_____

Whether it's a friendly conversation, helping with a task, a gift or something else, what could you do that they would appreciate?
_____
_____

**Closing Prayer:** Think about what's going on in their lives right now and take time to pray over their needs and concerns.

# Week 6

## Using Your Gifts as the Church

Using the gifts God has given us is about so much more than simply being moral or doing nice things for others. It is relying on the power of God to take our efforts and do more than we could accomplish on our own. When we respond to God's nudging or allow ourselves to do something uncomfortable so the work of the Lord can be done, we partner with the Holy Spirit in sacred work and extra space is created for lives to be changed. As a result, we are used by God in ways we never thought possible. One of the most powerful avenues for this is when fellow Christians rally together for the work of God's Kingdom. Whether you're outgoing or quiet, you tend to be a leader or more of a behind-the-scenes person, in this chapter we'll explore how all are a needed and integral part of the church. You'll be invited to explore how you organically fit into the church and you'll be challenged to consider how you can join your gifts with others to make even more of an impact.

**Day 36**

*¹² The human body has many parts, but the many parts make up one whole body. So it is with the body of Christ. ¹³ Some of us are Jews, some are Gentiles, some are slaves, and some are free. But we have all been baptized into one body by one Spirit, and we all share the same Spirit.*
- *1 Corinthians 12:12,13*

Like the different parts of the body, as the family of God, our diversity is not what separates us but what makes us whole. If you attend church, what groups of people are in your church family? If you don't attend a church, what are the groups of people that make up the majority of churches in your area (age, ethnicity, cultural background, job or skill set, religious/denominational background)? Don't rush. Take a moment to answer.

_____
_____
_____

Does this reflect your community? If not, what group(s) of people are missing? _____
_____
_____

Looking at the lists you just made, do you feel your local church(es) create space for all people within the community to find a place of worship and connection? If so, how? If not, what's missing? _____
_____
_____


**Closing Prayer:** What minority groups exist inside or outside the church? Think about any emotional, physical and/or spiritual needs they may have. Pray for them.

## Day 37

*14 Yes, the body has many different parts, not just one part. 15 If the foot says, "I am not a part of the body because I am not a hand," that does not make it any less a part of the body. 16 And if the ear says, "I am not part of the body because I am not an eye," would that make it any less a part of the body? 17 If the whole body were an eye, how would you hear? Or if your whole body were an ear, how would you smell anything?*
- *1 Corinthians 12:14-17*

We often don't notice the many parts of the body all working together behind the scenes and can take some things for granted. Think of all the people involved in just making a Sunday morning worship service happen (music, projection, prayers, flowers, coffee, scripture reading, bulletin, Sunday School teachers, greeters/ushers, etc.). See if you can name all the tasks that need to be completed for just Sunday worship to be properly prepared. _____

_____
_____

Beyond Sunday morning worship, what other ministries, activities or groups of the church can you think of?

_____
_____
_____

Sometimes those who work behind the scenes can feel as if their job isn't important. For example, in our scripture the ear believes it's not truly a part of the body because it thinks its work isn't as important as the eyes, but without it, the body cannot work as it was designed to! What unsung hero(s) of ministry within the church can you think of?

_____
_____

**Closing Prayer:** Consider the different people who serve in the church and thank God for them.

# Day 38

*[18] But our bodies have many parts, and God has put each part just where he wants it. [19] How strange a body would be if it had only one part! [20] Yes, there are many parts, but only one body.*
 - *1 Corinthians 12:18-20*

What do you feel is the role of a Christian in the life of the church? _____
_____
_____

What do you feel is your role in the life of the church?
_____
_____
_____

Is there anything holding you back from living in that role?
_____
_____
_____

If so, what can you begin doing about it? _____
_____
_____

**Closing Prayer:** Again, thank God for the gifts you've discovered throughout this book. Ask God to help you understand how he wants to use you through his church and ask him for the guidance and strength in dealing with anything holding you back.

## Day 39

*²¹ The eye can never say to the hand, "I don't need you." The head can't say to the feet, "I don't need you."*
*²² In fact, some parts of the body that seem weakest and least important are actually the most necessary. ²³ And the parts we regard as less honorable are those we clothe with the greatest care. So we carefully protect those parts that should not be seen, ²⁴ while the more honorable parts do not require this special care. So God has put the body together such that extra honor and care are given to those parts that have less dignity. ²⁵ This makes for harmony among the members, so that all the members care for each other.*
- *1 Corinthians 12:21-25*

Satan can make us feel as if we aren't talented enough, smart enough or been a Christian long enough to help serve through the church, but this is a lie! God has given you the specific gifts he has because he believes you're the one who can do good with them. God believes in you! Think about all the gifts you've discovered throughout this book. Now think about the ministries of the church (committees/boards, missions, classes, groups, actives, etc.). If you had your choice, which one(s) would you enjoy being a part of? _____

_____

Why would you enjoy serving in those ministries? _____

_____

Are there any ministries, groups or activities the church doesn't offer that you would like to be a part of? _____

_____

**Closing Prayer:** Ask the Lord to bless those ministries you've just listed and ask him to help you know how he might be calling you to serve there or else were.

## Day 40

$^{26}$ *If one part suffers, all the parts suffer with it, and if one part is honored, all the parts are glad.*
$^{27}$ *All of you together are Christ's body, and each of you is a part of it.*
- 1 Corinthians 12:26,27

Being an active part of the body of Christ, (i.e., the church) doesn't necessarily mean you have to be involved in lots of groups, classes, programs and committees/boards, or get roped into serving in a position you don't want. Being an active part of the body of Christ means connecting with other believers, worshiping together and finding joy in serving our God through who he made you to be. You are an important part of this! If even one person is missing or inactive, the body feels it and is incomplete.

In the same way, this 40-day journey only holds value if we do something with it! So, what are you ready to begin doing? Maybe it's attending worship more regularly. Maybe it's getting connected with a small group or class. Maybe it's taking a risk and committing to serving others in a new way, or volunteering to not just attend but help out with one of those groups, classes, programs or committees/boards. Maybe this book has been a confirmation and you're right where you need to be. God has uniquely designed you out of love and equipped you with spiritual gifts to find a deep sense of fulfillment in serving others. He has invited you to find fellowship with him and each other by being part of his body, the church. So, what are you going to do about it? What's your next step?

_____
_____
_____

**Closing Prayer:** Ask God to guide you in discovering where he wants you to serve through his church.

# What's Next?

Now that you've been through this journey, perhaps discovering more about who God made you to be, more about the kind of person you want to be and more about the gifts he's given you, there may be a sense of joy and excitement. I want to encourage you to do something with it before that passion dims. As the busyness of life begins to creep in, issues arise or doubts begin to surface in your mind, it can be easy to put your gifts on the back burner, assuming you'll get around to using them later.

Yet, now that this 40-day journey is over and you're thinking about what it looks like to use your gifts in perhaps new ways, we can also get discouraged because of self-doubt or fear that we won't be effective (or even fears we might just make a mess of things). But remember these two truths, the creator of the universe would not give you these gifts if he didn't believe you are the one that can do good with them, and Satan has no reason to fight you if he doesn't feel threated by you!

Therefore, pray about this, ask God to reveal where he wants you to do good, then be on the lookout for it. Don't overthink opportunities to serve or talk yourself out of them. Be willing to take a risk, step outside your comfort zone and if you think you can do good, try. Even if things don't quite turn out the way you were hoping, a little good is better than none at all. Also talk to your pastor, talk to church leaders you trust, talk to other Christians your close to, tell them what's on your heart and if they know of a place where your specific gifts could be used. When you open yourself up to God, you might be surprised what he puts in your path!

# Spiritual Gifts Survey

**DIRECTIONS:**

Remember, this is not a test, it's a survey. It is not intended to be a concrete analysis. It's intended to begin pointing you in the general direction of your spiritual gifts. Therefore, there are no right or wrong answers. When answering, it is best not to spend too much time on one statement. Usually your first reaction is best. Try not to answer how you would like others to think of you. The most honest answers will give you the most accurate results. Answer each statement, do not skip any and do not ask others how they think you should answer.

Answer each statement using the number system below (0-3) and write your number on the line provided or a scrap piece of paper. Only after you've answered every statement, turn to the Answer Sheet on page 58.

**0-Never   1-Seldom   2-Often   3-Typically**

___ 1. When there's confusion in a group I have a knack for helping to sort it out and get things done.
___ 2. I can often tell when someone's being genuine or trying to deceive me.
___ 3. I tend to be more positive and upbeat than most people.
___ 4. It's easy for me to talk with strangers about the love of Christ.
___ 5. In times of trouble my first reaction is to pray.
___ 6. I enjoy giving to an organization that makes a difference.
___ 7. I like to learn about scriptures that seem unclear.
___ 8. In group projects I notice who would be good at different tasks.
___ 9. I don't want to just talk about the needs of others, I want to do something about it.
___ 10. I often see potential in people, even when they don't see it in themselves.
___ 11. I show love by doing tasks for others.

___ 12. Helping others mature in their faith is very important to me.
___ 13. People have said they learn a lot from me.
___ 14. People often come to me for advice.
___ 15. I like being organized in my professional and personal life.
___ 16. I have such a deep sense of wrong and right, I feel driven to speak up about it even when it's uncomfortable.
___ 17. I don't give up easily when things become difficult.
___ 18. I enjoy talking to others about salvation.
___ 19. It's hard for me to understand how others struggle to trust God.
___ 20. Possessions aren't very important to me.
___ 21. I get excited about studying the Bible.
___ 22. I daydream about what it would be like to lead some groups.
___ 23. I tend to notice suffering in people, animals or nature more than most people.
___ 24. I often notice how God is trying to lead someone in their life.
___ 25. I enjoy volunteering or would like to volunteer more.
___ 26. I like to guide people into a deeper and more personal walk with God.
___ 27. I find teaching people new things fun.
___ 28. I often help people sort out difficult problems in their life.
___ 29. In groups, I enjoy being the one who helps things run smoothly.
___ 30. I can often tell someone's motives within the first few moments of talking to them.
___ 31. My typical reaction when others are struggling is to offer words of encouragement.
___ 32. It's easy for me to present the truth of Christ in a way that applies to different cultures and backgrounds.
___ 33. In dark times, I find it easy to rely on God.
___ 34. I often donate or give away items I know can help others.
___ 35. I like understanding not just what people think or believe, but why they believe it.
___ 36. Throughout my life, I've been in a leadership role multiple times, even if it seemed like a little thing at the time.

___ 37. The wrongs and injustice of this world bother me more than it seems to bother most people.
___ 38. I notice, in advance, how the different paths people or groups tend to take will affect them.
___ 39. I enjoy doing menial tasks.
___ 40. I like helping people see how scripture applies to their everyday lives.
___ 41. I enjoy helping people understand the Bible.
___ 42. I am often able to explain scriptures that seem unclear to others.
___ 43. I enjoy solving mysteries and/or puzzles.
___ 44. I notice when something evil is happening or when God is doing something great.
___ 45. I enjoy getting others to believe in themselves.
___ 46. I feel comfortable sharing the gospel message with nonbelievers.
___ 47. Staying in God's will is very important to me.
___ 48. I take tithing very seriously.
___ 49. I like hearing different points of view on scripture and thinking about them.
___ 50. I often think about what I would do different if I were in charge.
___ 51. I'm passionately driven to help the hurting, abused and neglected.
___ 52. I think a lot about where a person, group, ministry or organization will be in a few years if they continue on in the way they are.
___ 53. I'm a behind-the-scenes kind of person.
___ 54. I find myself giving spiritual direction to others.
___ 55. I'm good at explaining things and it tends to help others when I do.
___ 56. When a person has a problem, I often guide them to a Biblical solution which brings them clarity.

# Defining Your Spiritual Gifts

To help us along our journey, we've been using the three places traditionally understood where scripture mentions spiritual gifts (Romans 12:6-8, 1 Corinthians 12:7-31 and Ephesians 4:11-13). To help understand these gifts better, below is a brief explanation of each gift. Please note that some translations of the Bible may use slightly different English words in referring to some spiritual gifts.

**Administration** – The Greek word used here, *kubernaō* has a naval undertone to it, referring to someone piloting, navigating or directing a ship; similar to how groups of believers need both clear direction and someone to help them navigate that path. It carries with it the idea of organizing groups of people within the church, organizing church business and/or organizing tasks. The person with this spiritual gift often has the ability to effectively empower others by helping a church or group develop both goals and steps for moving towards those goals. (1 Cor. 12:28)

**Discernment** – The Greek word used here, *diakrisis* describes someone who has the ability to distinguish between right and wrong motives, someone who instinctively notices falsehoods when it's not obvious. In teachings, conversations and situations, the person with this spiritual gift can often distinguish between the influence of God and Satan. It is also not uncommon for this person to intuitively distinguish between a well-intended person, human error and human ego. (1 Cor. 12:10)

**Encouragement/Exhortation**– The Greek word used here, *parakaleō* means to exhort, encourage or comfort. The person with this spiritual gift has a yearning to come alongside people in times of confusion or need. This person often offers council and motivation, helping others to see as well as focus on the courage, strength and hope that can only come from God. (Rom. 12:8)

**Evangelism** – The Greek word used here, *euaggelistēs* means evangelist, preacher of the gospel or bringer/messenger of good news. The person with this spiritual gift is keenly aware of the eternal destinations of those around them and has a deep seeded passion to help non-Christians understand the saving grace of Jesus Christ. For this person, the eternal souls of others weigh heavy on them and they feel a call to help others take the necessary steps to accept Christ in their hearts. (Eph. 4:11)

**Faith** – The Greek word used here, *pistis* means faith, assurance, belief or fidelity. This carries with it a notion of confidence, assurance and trust in Christ. The person with this spiritual gift is often marked with a deeper reliance on God than most in their personal lives, a strong belief that the teachings of scripture are the guideposts of all life's decisions and a deep seeded personal assurance that all of God's promises will be fulfilled through the power of the Holy Spirit. This person continuously reminds the church to keep all it does focused on Christ. They also help other believers remain faithful and obedient during times of difficulty or apathy. (1 Cor. 12:9)

**Giving** – The Greek word used here, *metadidōmi* simply means to give or to impart, but this word is partnered with another, *haplotēs* which means to give sincerely, to give without being self-seeking or to give generously. The person with this spiritual gift sees giving as an investment in the lives of others. They clearly see how it can impact the work of God's Kingdom and they find personal fulfillment in being one of the pieces of that puzzle, bringing that ministry to life. The person with this gift views funds, time and energy simply as tools God has lent to us and calls us to use. (Rom. 12:8)

**Knowledge** – The Greek word used here, *gno'sis* means knowing or understanding and refers to giving words of knowledge. The person with this spiritual gift has an ability to explain scriptures in a way that makes it understandable to others, apply the truths of the Bible to life situations and explain scriptures that may seem unclear. (1 Cor. 12:8)

**Leadership** – The Greek word used here, *proistēmi* means to lead, to rule or to preside, this carries with it the notion of protecting, caring for and motivating. The person with this spiritual gift has the ability to inspire others and lead them towards a vision. This person is often motivated by helping others achieve goals and their focus is often on how the group's efforts will build up the church or meet needs. (Rom. 12:8, 1 Cor. 12:28)

**Mercy** – The Greek word used here, *eleeō* means to be compassionate, have pity on or to show mercy in either word or deed. The person with this spiritual gift tends to be patient and compassionate. They intuitively notice suffering in the world, suffering in others and feel a strong desire to be the hands and feet of Christ in relieving that suffering. (Rom. 12:8)

**Prophecy** – The Greek word used here, *prophēteia* means prediction or to prophesy. The person with this gift can both build up the body of Christ through seeing potential in others they don't always see in themselves as well as lead the church through conviction of sin. This person often notices what the broader consequences for the future will be, if a group or individual continues with their actions or approach. If something needs to change, they may also have insights for moving towards God's will. (1 Cor. 12:10; Rom. 12:6)

**Serving/Helps** – The Greek word used here, *diakonia* means to attend to, minister to or to serve. This is where the church gets the word deacon. The person with this spiritual gift enjoys assisting in caring for most any need in the church, accomplishing tasks and serving those in need. This gift is broad enough to include many people, from those who find fulfillment in accomplishing church business, to those who have a strong desire to care for the destitute, abused and abandoned. This person is often involved in (or would like to be involved in) multiple volunteer opportunities and finds joy in serving others. (1 Cor. 12:28; Rom. 12:7)

**Shepherding** – The Greek word used here, *poimēn* means a pastor or shepherd. The person with this spiritual gift looks out for the spiritual welfare of others. They instinctively nurture, guide and protect the people of God. They feel an obligation to care for their spiritual needs and often see those under their care as family. (Eph. 4:11)

**Teaching** – The Greek word used here, *didaskalos* means to teach, to master or doctrine. The person with this spiritual gift is able to bring an understanding and depth to other's faith walk by helping them comprehend scripture and clarify church doctrine. It is through effectively sharing the truth of the scriptures and the teachings of the church that they are able to help instill a stronger theology in others. (1 Cor. 12:28; Rom. 12:7; Eph. 4:11)

**Wisdom** – The Greek word used here, *sophia* refers to speaking or uttering words of wisdom. The person with this spiritual gift has the ability to speak clarity based on God's commands and teachings through scripture. This gift often cuts through rationalization, confusion and manipulation to help vivify a righteous perspective in conversations or situation. Where the gift of knowledge may be referred to as a more scholarly gift, wisdom may be referred to as the life application or street smarts gift. (1 Cor. 12:8)

# Answer Sheet

You're welcome to remove this page, make a copy of it or use a scrap piece of paper. If removing this page or copying, fold along the dotted line so the names of each gift is hidden, this will help reduce the temptation to change your answer. *Only after* you have answered each statement add your total at the end of each line (see the example below).

## Example

| Faith | (5) 1 | + | (19) 3 | + | (33) 0 | + | (47) 2 | = | 6 |

## Answer Key

|  | | | | | | | | |
|---|---|---|---|---|---|---|---|---|
| Administration | (1) | + | (15) | + | (29) | + | (43) | = |
| Discernment | (2) | + | (16) | + | (30) | + | (44) | = |
| Encouragement/ Exhortation | (3) | + | (17) | + | (31) | + | (45) | = |
| Evangelism | (4) | + | (18) | + | (32) | + | (46) | = |
| Faith | (5) | + | (19) | + | (33) | + | (47) | = |
| Giving | (6) | + | (20) | + | (34) | + | (48) | = |
| Knowledge | (7) | + | (21) | + | (35) | + | (49) | = |
| Leadership | (8) | + | (22) | + | (36) | + | (50) | = |
| Mercy | (9) | + | (23) | + | (37) | + | (51) | = |
| Prophecy | (10) | + | (24) | + | (38) | + | (52) | = |
| Serving/Helps | (11) | + | (25) | + | (39) | + | (53) | = |
| Shepherding | (12) | + | (26) | + | (40) | + | (54) | = |
| Teaching | (13) | + | (27) | + | (41) | + | (55) | = |
| Wisdom | (14) | + | (28) | + | (42) | + | (56) | = |

*Go to page 59 to better understand your answers.*

Due to the diversity of definition and application, some spiritual gifts are not included in this survey.

## Primary Spiritual Gifts

There are often a group of 1-3 spiritual gifts that rank higher than others when taking a spiritual gifts survey. These are typically your primary spiritual gifts, ones that often rank high most of your life and can speak directly into your passions and personality. What are your primary spiritual gift(s)?

_____   _____   _____

## Secondary Spiritual Gifts

There can also be a second cluster of 1-3 gifts, that are close in how they rank, are not as high as your primary gifts, but tend to be higher than the rest, these are your secondary gifts. These gifts may change as God gives you different abilities and passions for what's happening in your life at that time. What are your secondary spiritual gift(s)?

_____   _____   _____

*Go to page 53 for a general definition of your gifts.*

# Acknowledgements

A special thanks to
*Travis Boline*
for helping with scripture selection.

A special thanks to
*The Beans and Bibles Coffee Shop Church of Havana, FL.,
Connie Kummer,
Karen Hamilton,
Karen Stansberry
& Amy Cain*
for helping with book review and editing.

# Bibliography

*The following Public Domain publications were used to assist in translating Greek words in the "Defining Your Spiritual Gifts" section.*

*King James Concordance.* Derivative Work, 1769.
Strong, James. *Strong's Hebrew and Greek Dictionaries. n.p.*1890.

Made in the USA
Columbia, SC
24 December 2021